Marketing for Youtubers and Influencers

Index

"Marketing for Youtubers and Influencers" is a complete book that offers an overview of the world of influencer marketing and how it can be applied by Youtubers and Influencers to build their personal brands, create attractive content, increase their follower base and generate income from their social networks.

The book begins by introducing the concept of Influencer Marketing and why it is important for Youtubers and Influencers. It then offers guidance on how to build a strong personal brand, define your value proposition, and create a consistent brand image.

The book also introduces techniques for creating successful content on YouTube, including how to identify topics of interest to your audience, create compelling content, and optimize your videos for SEO.

Another important topic covered in the book is how to negotiate with brands to get profitable partnerships and sponsorships, as well as guidance on how to engage your community, deal with negative comments, and manage reputation crises.

The book also explores strategies for monetizing content and maximizing opportunities to make money from social media. Finally, it offers an overview of analyzing data and metrics to measure success and improve marketing strategies, as well as exploring emerging trends in influencer marketing and how to prepare for the future of the industry.

"Marketing for Youtubers and Influencers" is a practical and accessible guide that offers Youtubers and Influencers the tools they need to build their personal brands, create successful content, grow their follower base, and generate income from their social networks.

1: Introduction to Influencer Marketing

What is Influencer Marketing

Influencer marketing is a form of marketing that focuses on utilizing the influence of well-known and influential people, such as YouTubers and influencers, to promote products or services. The goal of influencer marketing is to increase brand awareness, build trust, and increase sales.

Influencers are people who have loyal followers on their social media platforms and can have a significant impact on their followers' buying decisions. With influencer marketing, brands work with these influencers to reach their target audiences, promote their products or services, and create brand awareness.

One of the main advantages of influencer marketing is its ability to reach highly specific audiences. With the help of data analytics tools, brands can identify influencers who are popular among the target audience they want to reach, and then work with those influencers to create relevant content that resonates with that audience.

In addition, influencer marketing is often seen as more authentic than other forms of advertising. People rely on recommendations from people they consider authentic and trustworthy, rather than generic brand ads. By working with influencers who already have a loyal audience, brands can leverage that trust and authenticity to promote their products or services in a way that feels more organic and natural.

Influencer marketing can also be more profitable than other forms of advertising. While working with influencers can be expensive, the costs can still be lower than other forms of advertising, such as TV or radio ads. In addition, brands can benefit from the long-term effect of influencer recommendations, which can continue to generate sales long after the content has been posted.

However, it is important to remember that influencer marketing is not a quick and easy solution to all marketing problems. It is important to identify the right influencer for the right audience and work with them to create authentic and valuable content that resonates with the audience. It is also important to be transparent about the nature of partnerships and sponsorships and to ensure that all influencer marketing practices comply with advertising guidelines.

Influencer marketing is a form of marketing that involves collaborating with influential people to promote products or services. It is an effective way to reach highly specific audiences and can be more authentic and profitable than other forms of advertising. However, it is important to remember that influencer marketing is not a quick and easy solution to all marketing problems and requires a careful strategy to ensure long-term success.

In terms of benefits for companies, Influencer Marketing can bring meaningful results, such as: increased brand awareness, increased traffic to the website, increased sales and lead generation. Influencer Marketing also allows companies to more segment their target audience, as they can choose influencers who match the interests and characteristics of their potential customers. In addition, influencer marketing can be more effective than other marketing methods since many consumers trust influencers' opinions and consider them more authentic and honest than traditional advertising.

For influencers, influencer marketing can be an opportunity to monetize your audience and your content. Influencers can receive payment in cash, products, or services in exchange for their collaboration with a brand. In addition, influencers can use Influencer Marketing to become better known and increase their reach, which can lead to new opportunities for collaboration with other brands and greater success in the world of digital marketing.

To conclude, Influencer Marketing is a marketing strategy that relies on collaboration between companies and influencers to promote products and services. This strategy has been gaining increased importance in recent years, due to the growing popularity of influencers and its impact on consumers' purchase decisions. However, it is important that companies choose the right influencers for their brand and that influencers maintain an authentic relationship with their audience, so that Influencer Marketing is effective.

How Influencer Marketing Works for Youtubers and Influencers

Influencer Marketing is a marketing strategy that has been gaining increased importance in recent years. This strategy involves collaboration between a brand and a digital influencer, such as a YouTuber, with the goal of reaching a specific audience and promoting a product or service.

For influencer marketing to be effective, it is important that the brand chooses an influencer whose audience aligns with the brand's target audience. This means that the influencer should have followers who have similar interests, needs, or characteristics to the brand's potential customers.

By collaborating with an influencer, the brand can leverage the influence they have on their followers and use that to promote their brand. This is usually done by creating sponsored content, such as videos on Youtube or posts on social networks, where the influencer talks about the brand's product or service.

One of the main advantages of Influencer Marketing is its ability to reach a highly targeted audience. Because the influencer already has a loyal and engaged audience, the brand's message can be delivered more effectively than through traditional advertising. In addition, because the influencer has already built a relationship of trust with their followers, the promotion of products or services may seem more authentic and less invasive.

However, it is important for influencers to be transparent with their followers about the fact that they are promoting a product or service. This transparency can be achieved using hashtags such as #publi or #ad in sponsored posts. It is important for influencers to maintain the integrity of their personal brand and avoid promoting products or services that don't align with their personal values or interests.

Another important aspect of Influencer Marketing is the measurement of results. Brands should be prepared to invest in analytics and monitoring tools that allow them to assess the impact of their influencer campaigns. This includes monitoring audience engagement, website traffic, and sales generated by the campaign.

Influencer Marketing is a marketing strategy that involves collaboration between a brand and a digital influencer to promote a product or service. For the strategy to be effective, it is important that the brand chooses an influencer that has an audience aligned with its target audience and that influencers are transparent with their followers about the fact that they are promoting a product or service. In addition, it is important for brands to invest in analytics and monitoring tools to assess the impact of their influencer campaigns.

To succeed in influencer marketing, it is important for YouTubers and influencers to partner with brands that are aligned with their content and have an audience like yours. This partnership can be done in several ways, such as:

Sponsored posts: In this format, the youtuber or influencer publishes a video or photo in which he mentions or uses the brand's product or service and receives remuneration in return.

Affiliate programs: In this model, the youtuber or influencer promotes a product or service through an affiliate link and earns a commission whenever someone makes a purchase through your link.

Events: Youtubers and influencers can be invited to events or promotional campaigns, where they have the opportunity to get to know the brand and its target audience.

Long-term partnerships: Some brands choose to enter into long-term partnerships with YouTubers and influencers, where they become brand ambassadors and collaborate on various campaigns over time.

Regardless of the format chosen, it is important that the partnership is transparent and that the youtuber or influencer makes it clear to his audience that it is a sponsored publication. This can be done in a variety of ways, such as using the hashtag #publi or #ad in the title or description of the video or mentioning that the content is sponsored during the video itself.

It's important to remember that authenticity is key in influencer marketing. YouTubers and influencers need to maintain their identity and their voice, and should only accept partnerships with brands that are genuinely relevant to their audience. Otherwise, they may end up losing the trust and respect of their followers.

Another important aspect to consider is the measurement of results. It is essential that youtubers and influencers track the performance of their sponsored posts, to ensure that they are achieving the goals agreed with the brand. For this, they can use data analysis tools, such as Google Analytics or YouTube Analytics, which allow you to evaluate the number of views, likes, comments and shares.

In summary, influencer marketing is an increasingly popular strategy among brands, which seek to connect with their audiences through youtubers and influencers. For YouTubers and influencers, this can be an opportunity to monetize their content and connect with new brands and audiences. However, it is important that these partnerships are authentic, transparent, and aligned with the influencer's identity and values.

Why Influencer Marketing Is Important for Youtubers and Influencers

Influencer Marketing is a marketing strategy that has grown a lot in recent years, especially for youtubers and influencers. But why is this strategy so important to them? In this text, we will explore the reasons.

Firstly, Influencer Marketing allows YouTubers and influencers to reach a larger and more engaged audience. By working with brands and promoting their products or services, these influencers have the opportunity to expose their brand to a wider audience. In addition, this audience is often more engaged than that found in other types of marketing. This is because followers of youtubers and influencers are often loyal fans and trust your recommendations.

Secondly, Influencer Marketing can be an important source of income for youtubers and influencers. By promoting products or services on their channels, they can make money from sponsorships and affiliate deals. These partnerships are an effective way to monetize your content and generate additional revenue.

In addition, working with brands through Influencer Marketing can increase the credibility and reputation of YouTubers and influencers. This is because they are associating your brand with other trusted and respected brands. This helps increase followers' trust in your recommendations and increases your credibility as an influencer.

Another reason why influencer marketing is important for YouTubers and influencers is that it can help increase your reach and visibility. When an influencer works with a brand, it often results in greater exposure on social media channels and other media. This, in turn, can attract new followers and increase the overall visibility of your channel.

Influencer Marketing can help YouTubers and influencers create a more engaged community around their content. By working with brands, they can encourage follower participation through sweepstakes, contests, and other activities. This can help create a more active and engaged community around your channel, which can lead to greater engagement and loyalty from followers.

Influencer Marketing is important for YouTubers and influencers because it allows them to reach a larger and more engaged audience, generate additional revenue, increase their credibility and reputation, increase their reach and visibility, and create a more engaged community around their content. For these reasons, it is essential that YouTubers and influencers consider Influencer Marketing as part of their overall marketing strategy.

In addition, influencer marketing allows YouTubers and influencers to be compensated for their content creation work and for their ability to reach and influence their audience. With the increased demand for influencers, many brands are willing to pay for sponsored posts and partnerships if they are relevant to their audience.

Another important aspect of influencer marketing is that it can help YouTubers and influencers increase their visibility and reach online. By working with brands and other influential personalities, they can attract new followers and expand their audience. In addition, influencer marketing can lead to opportunities for collaboration and career growth, such as invitations to events and conferences, or even proposals to launch your own product or product line.

Finally, influencer marketing allows YouTubers and influencers to be recognized as opinion leaders in their niches and industries. They can build a reputation as experts in their field and be seen as reliable and reputable references for their followers. This can increase your influence and authority in the online and offline world.

In summary, influencer marketing is an effective strategy for YouTubers and influencers who want to build and maintain a loyal and engaged audience, while generating revenue and increasing their visibility and authority online. By creating authentic and relevant content and working with brands aligned with their values and interests, influencers can stand out and thrive in a highly competitive market.

Chapter 2: Building Your Personal Brand

Identifying your audience

Identifying the audience is a crucial step for any marketing strategy, including for Youtubers and Influencers. Knowing who your target audience is and what they're looking for is key to creating relevant and compelling content that can generate meaningful engagement with the audience.

To identify your audience, it is important to first define the theme or niche of your channel or profile. After that, you need to conduct research to better understand your target audience and interests. Here are some steps that can help you identify your audience:

Set the theme of your channel or profile.

Before you start identifying your audience, you need to clearly define the theme or niche of your channel or profile. It's important that you have a clear focus in terms of content to ensure your audience knows what to expect from your channel or profile.

Research your current audience

Analyze your current audience to gain valuable insights into your audience. You can use social media analytics tools to get demographics, information about your followers, interests, and behavior. With this data, you can create a profile of your current audience.

Analyze the competition.

Look at competing channels and profiles and look at the type of content they are producing and who your audience is. This can help you identify niche segmentation opportunities that the competition isn't taking advantage of.

Create personas of your target audience.

Once you have gathered information about your current audience and analyzed the competition, create personas for your target audience. Personas are detailed profiles of your audience, which include information such as age, gender, interests, behavior, buying habits, and more. These profiles help you better understand what your audience wants and needs.

Conduct market research.

Market research is another way to gain insight into your target audience. You can create surveys and send them to your followers, as well as your customers or potential customers, and get information about their interests, preferences, and opinions.

Monitor feedback and metrics.

Finally, monitor feedback and metrics from your channel or profile to get real-time feedback on your content. Observe your followers' interactions and comments on your posts and use social media metrics to analyze the performance of your posts and your channel or profile in general.

By identifying your audience, you can create content that resonates with your target audience and develop a more effective marketing strategy for your channel or profile. It is important to remember that your audience isn't static and ever evolving, so it's important to continue to monitor and update your audience profile on a regular basis.

Once the audience has been identified, it is important to get to know them well so you can create content that meets their needs and interests. For this, it is necessary to conduct research and data analysis to understand the demographic profile, online behavior, and consumption preferences of the audience.

Some ways to accomplish this are:

Market research: It is possible to conduct market research to obtain information about the target audience, including age, gender, location, interests, and consumption habits. This can be done through online questionnaires, interviews or focus groups.

Data analytics: Social media platforms and Google Analytics provide insight into audience behavior, such as the time they spend on each platform, the pages they visit most often, and the keywords they use to find content. This can help to better understand the needs and interests of the audience.

Social media monitoring: Observing and analyzing followers' interactions with content can provide valuable insight into what they like, what they comment on and share, and how they respond to diverse types of content. This can help fine-tune the content to meet the needs of the audience.

Direct feedback: Establishing an open communication channel with the audience, whether through comments on social media, email, or other forms of communication, can provide direct feedback on what the audience likes and dislikes, and what they would like to see.

By better understanding the audience, you can create more engaging and relevant content, increase audience engagement and loyalty, and build a strong community around the influencer's channel or profile.

Defining your value proposition

Defining your value proposition is a crucial step in marketing for youtubers and influencers. Your value proposition is the way you differentiate yourself from other content creators by showing your followers what makes your channel or profile unique and valuable.

An effective value proposition is made up of three main elements: the value offering, the target audience, and differentiation. Let us explore each of these elements in more detail.

The value offer refers to what you are offering to your followers. This can include the content you create, the tone of your message, or the type of interaction you have with your followers. The value offering should solve a specific problem or meet a need of your audience.

The target audience is the person for whom you are creating your content. It's important to understand the demographic and behavioral characteristics of your target audience, including age, interests, location, and issues they face. The better you know your audience, the more effective your value proposition will be.

Differentiation is the way in which you stand out from other youtubers and influencers who address the same target audience as you. Differentiation can be based on anything from the unique personality of your channel or profile to the superior quality of your content.

To define your value proposition, start by answering these questions:

What do I offer my followers?

Who is my audience? What problems do they face?

How is my content different from other creators' content?

By answering these questions, you will have a clearer idea of what makes your channel or profile unique and valuable. With this information, you can create a clear and compelling value proposition for your followers.

It is important to remember that your value proposition is not something fixed and immutable. As you grow and evolve as a content creator, your value proposition can also change. Stay open to adjusting your value proposition as your audience grows and their needs change.

In addition, it is important to communicate your value proposition clearly throughout your content and interaction with your followers. Make sure your followers understand what you have to offer and how you differentiate yourself from other content creators. This will help strengthen your relationship with your followers and grow your fan base.

In summary, defining your value proposition is a major step for youtubers and influencers who want to stand out in the competitive content creation market. By understanding your value offering, target audience, and differentiation, you can create a clear and compelling value proposition that connects with your followers and encourages them to keep following your content.

Once you have defined your value proposition, it's time to communicate it clearly and convincingly to your audience. This can be done through different channels such as your homepage, channel description, videos, social media posts, and other marketing materials.

It is important to remember that communicating your value proposition should be consistent across all the channels you are present on. This helps create a strong and cohesive brand image, which is critical to success in influencer marketing.

When creating your value proposition message, it is important to think about what makes it unique relative to other YouTubers or influencers in your niche. What do you offer that others do not? What are your skills, experiences, and values that make you stand out?

It's also important to think about how your value proposition can benefit your audience. What problem are you solving or what need are you meeting for your followers? How can you help them achieve their goals or improve their lives?

Once you have a clear and compelling message of your value proposition, you can start incorporating it into your marketing materials. Make sure your message is clear and easy to understand and use words and images that resonate with your audience.

In addition, it is important to regularly update your value proposition message as your career evolves and your audience grows and changes. Be open to feedback and adjustments of your message to ensure it remains relevant and appealing to your audience.

Remember that communicating your value proposition is only one aspect of influencer marketing. It is also important to provide high-quality, engaging content to your audience, build relationships with brands and other influencers in your niche, and continue to grow and adapt in an ever-changing landscape of digital marketing.

Creating a consistent brand image

Creating a consistent brand image is critical to the success of a YouTuber or influencer. Brand image is the perception that the audience has of the content creator, and it is important to ensure that this perception is positive and consistent. This helps build a loyal and compelling fan base for brands looking to collaborate with influencers.

The first step in creating a consistent brand image is to define the brand identity. This includes choosing a color palette, typography, and a logo that reflects the personality of the YouTuber or influencer. It is important that these elements are used on all platforms where the content creator is present, including social networks, website, and YouTube videos.

In addition, the message that the youtuber or influencer is trying to convey should be clear and coherent across all platforms. This includes the type of content that is created, the tone of voice used in videos and social media posts, and even the way the YouTuber or influencer interacts with their audience. This consistency helps create an emotional connection with the audience and build a loyal fan base.

Another essential element in creating a consistent brand image is the choice of a niche or area of expertise. This helps establish the YouTuber or influencer as an authority on a specific subject and attracting an audience that is interested in that topic. For example, a YouTuber who is enthusiastic about cooking might specialize in vegan recipes and attract a specific audience that shares that interest.

It is important to remember that brand image is more than just visual elements and consistent messaging. The way the youtuber or influencer interacts with their audience, how they respond to comments and messages, and the way they behave outside the camera are also essential elements in building a positive and consistent brand image.

Creating a consistent brand image is critical to the success of a YouTuber or influencer. This includes defining the brand identity, having a clear and coherent message, choosing a niche or area of expertise, and interacting with the audience in a way that is authentic and consistent with the brand image. With a strong and consistent brand image, a YouTuber or influencer can build a loyal and attractive fan base for brands seeking influencer collaborations.

To maintain a consistent brand image, it is important to carefully choose the colors, fonts, and visual elements that will be used on your social media channels and platforms. These elements should be consistent across your online and offline presence.

In addition, it is important to maintain a consistent tone of voice throughout your communications. If you are often funny and laid-back in your videos, but formal and professional in your social media posts, this can cause confusion in your audience. Set the tone of voice you want to use and make sure it stays consistent across all your communications.

Another important aspect is the content you create. Make sure your videos and social media posts are aligned with your brand image and your value proposition. This helps reinforce the message you are trying to convey and maintain a strong and consistent brand image.

It's also important to monitor what people are saying about you and your brand on social media and other channels. If you encounter negative comments or constructive criticism, take them into consideration and make the necessary changes to improve your brand image and the value you are offering your audience.

Finally, remember that building a consistent brand image is an ongoing process. As your brand grows and evolves, your brand image must also evolve to keep up. Be open to feedback and change and be willing to adjust your branding strategy if necessary to maintain a strong and consistent brand image.

In short, creating a consistent brand image is critical to the success of any YouTuber or influencer. By defining your value proposition, identifying your audience, choosing your visual elements carefully, maintaining a consistent tone of voice, and creating content aligned with your brand image, you can build a strong online presence and a loyal audience. And by monitoring your brand image and being open to feedback and change, you can continue to evolve and grow as a successful YouTuber or influencer.

Chapter 3:

Successful Content

on YouTube

Identifying topics of interest to your audience

Identifying topics of interest to your audience is one of the most important parts of marketing for youtubers and influencers. Without understanding what your audience is interested in, it's hard to create content that will attract and keep their attention. In this article, we'll explore some strategies for identifying topics relevant to your audience.

Channel data analysis

One of the most effective ways to understand what your audience is interested in is to analyze data from your YouTube channel or other social media platforms you're active on. The data can provide insight into the type of content that receives the most views, comments, likes, and shares. They can also help you understand the demographics of your audience, including age, gender, geographic location, and interests.

By analyzing this data, you can identify the content topics that resonate most with your audience and create more content in that direction. Plus, by better understanding who your audience is, you can create content that speaks directly to them.

Keyword research

Another strategy for identifying topics of interest to your audience is to conduct keyword research relevant to your niche. Keyword research tools like Google Keyword Planner can provide insight into the words and phrases people are using to search for content related to your niche.

By understanding the keywords your audience is using, you can create SEO-optimized content that will attract organic traffic to your channel or social profile. In addition, keyword research can help identify relevant and emerging content trends that you can capitalize on.

Engagement with your audience

Engaging with your audience is one of the best ways to understand what they're interested in. It is important to be present in the comments of your channel or social profile and answer the questions of your followers. In addition, you can conduct research on social networks to better understand the needs and interests of your audience.

By actively engaging with your audience, you can identify the topics that interest them most and create content that meets their needs and wants.

Follow-up of influencers and thought leaders.

Influencers and thought leaders in your niche can provide valuable insights into the topics your audience is interested in. Tracking your social media channels and looking at the type of content they're producing can help identify relevant content trends.

In addition, you can monitor the conversations that are happening around these influencers to better understand what your audience is discussing and interested in. By being aware of the conversations that are happening in your niche, you can create content that is relevant and timely.

Identifying topics of interest to your audience is crucial to marketing success for youtubers and influencers.

To identify topics of interest to your audience, it is important that Youtubers and Influencers are always attentive to the comments and feedback of their followers. This can be done through social networks, including YouTube itself, as well as through market research and data analysis.

In addition, it is important to be up to date on the issues of the moment, as well as the trends of your niche. This can be done by reading specialized news and blogs, participating in forums and discussion groups, and following other content creators in the same niche.

Another effective strategy is the use of keyword analysis tools, which allow you to discover the terms and phrases most searched for by users in relation to a particular topic. In this way, Youtubers and Influencers can create content that meets the needs and interests of their audience.

However, it's important to remember that content creation shouldn't just be based on momentary fads or trends, but rather on creating authentic, quality content that consistently meets the needs and interests of your audience.

Therefore, it is important that Youtubers and Influencers make a careful analysis of the needs and interests of their audience, considering factors such as age, gender, geographic location, preferences and consumption habits. That way, they can create content that resonates with their audience and helps build a solid base of loyal and engaged followers.

Finally, it is important to remember that the process of identifying topics of interest to the audience is continuous and must always be adapted to changes in the market and in the interests of users. Therefore, Youtubers and Influencers should always be attentive and open to feedback and suggestions from their followers, and willing to change and evolve according to the needs of their audience.

Creating compelling, high-quality content

Creating quality content is essential for any Youtuber or influencer who wants to grow on the platform. With the growing competition and the increase in the amount of content creators, it is necessary to stand out with materials that are attractive and relevant to the target audience.

Compelling content can be defined as something that holds the viewer's or follower's attention. For this to happen, the content needs to be original, have a different approach or a unique perspective on a topic. In addition, it is important that it is produced with quality, both in editing and in image and sound capture.

Below, we present some tips to help create compelling, high-quality content:

Know your audience: It is essential to understand who the target audience of your channel or profile is. Knowing your preferences, needs and interests allows you to create content that is relevant and attractive to this audience.

Plan your content: Before you start recording, plan the ideas and topics you want to cover. This helps prevent repetitions and ensures that you are offering consistent and complete content.

Invest in equipment: Having quality equipment such as cameras, microphones, and lighting is essential to producing high-quality content. Try to invest in equipment suitable for the type of content you produce.

Work on editing: Editing is an important part of content production, as it is what gives rhythm and cohesion to the material. Invest time in editing to ensure that the final content is in line with your audience's expectations.

Be creative: Don't be afraid to experiment and differentiate yourself from other creators. Try to offer a unique point of view on a topic or explore different formats for your videos or posts.

Be consistent: It's important to maintain a regular frequency of posts to maintain engagement with your audience. Be consistent in posts and try to offer quality content whenever possible.

In summary, creating attractive, high-quality content is a key part of marketing for Youtubers and influencers. It is necessary to be attentive to the needs of the audience and invest in appropriate equipment and in the editing of the material to ensure that the final content is of quality. In addition, it is important to be creative and consistent in publications to maintain the interest of the target audience.

In addition, it is important that the content is authentic and reflects the personality and values of the influencer. Followers are drawn to authenticity and transparency, and superficial or false content can drive away the audience.

Another aspect to consider is consistency in content publishing. It's important to maintain a regular schedule of posts to maintain audience interest and engagement. Influencers should evaluate their ability to produce high-quality content and set a realistic posting frequency.

Finally, it is critical to keep up with trends and audience feedback to continuously adjust and improve the content produced. Social media platforms offer a variety of analytics tools that can help influencers better understand their audience's behavior and identify which types of content are most popular.

In short, creating compelling, high-quality content is critical to influencers' success on social media platforms. Influencers should take into consideration their audience, define their value proposition, and create authentic and consistent content that reflects their personality and values. In addition, they should evaluate their ability to produce content regularly and use analytics tools to continually improve their content and increase their engagement with the audience.

Optimizing your videos for SEO

Video optimization for SEO (Search Engine Optimization) is a fundamental step to the success of a YouTube channel or an influencer profile. This is because, with good SEO, videos are more likely to appear in the search results of search engines, such as Google, and thus attract more views and increase brand visibility.

To start optimizing your videos, you need to think about keywords that are relevant to your content. Keywords are the terms that people use to find what they are looking for on the internet, and should be chosen based on the topics covered in your videos. Use keyword research tools to identify the ones that are most popular and relevant to your niche.

Once you've identified the keywords, it's time to use them in the video title and description. The title should be clear and concise, and contain the main keyword early on. The description should be more detailed, including the keywords related to the topic and a brief synopsis of the content covered. It is also important to include relevant links and tags that help in identifying the content.

In addition to the title and description, tags are also a key part of SEO optimization. They help identify the themes of the video and rank it for search results. Use keywords related to the theme of the video and variations of them, including common spelling mistakes. This can help capture a larger share of misspelled searches and still rank the video correctly.

Optimizing video thumbnails is also important to grab users' attention and increase the chances of clicks. Thumbnails should be relevant to the video content and include compelling visual elements. Custom thumbnails tend to have more clicks than automatic thumbnails generated by YouTube.

Another factor that can help in optimizing videos is the watch time. The more time a user spends watching your video, the greater the engagement and, consequently, the relevance of your content. Therefore, it is important to produce videos with relevant and quality content, which hold the viewer's attention and maintain interest over time.

Don't forget to promote your content on social media and other channels relevant to your niche. The more shares and views a video have, the greater the relevance of your content to search engines.

Video optimization for SEO is a crucial part of success on YouTube and other video platforms. By choosing relevant keywords, using appropriate tags, and producing quality content, you can increase the visibility of your channel or influencer profile and attract an ever-growing audience.

Another important technique is choosing the right keywords. Keywords are the terms that people use to search for content on YouTube. By including relevant keywords in your video's title, description, and tags, you increase your chances of being found by anyone who is looking for content related to your topic.

To find the right keywords, you can use keyword research tools such as Google AdWords Keyword Planner or TubeBuddy. These tools provide a list of relevant keywords based on your topic and show how often people search for them. You can also search for popular videos related to your theme and see what keywords they used in their titles and descriptions.

Another important technique for optimizing videos is the use of attractive thumbnails. The thumbnail is the image that appears along with the title of the video on the YouTube search results page and is also displayed in related video suggestions. An attractive thumbnail can grab the viewer's attention and increase the chances of someone clicking and watching your video.

In addition, it is important to keep in mind the length of the video. While there is no general rule for optimal video length, many marketing experts recommend keeping videos between 3 and 5 minutes, as this matches the average attention span of a viewer. However, if your content requires more time, don't be afraid to extend the duration of the video. The important thing is to keep the viewer interested all the time, creating high-quality and engaging content.

In summary, optimizing your videos for SEO can significantly increase your chances of being found by your target audience. By following the above techniques, you can create more relevant and engaging videos, increasing your visibility on YouTube and, in turn, improving your personal marketing as a Youtuber or Influencer. Always remember that quality content is the key to success on any social media platform.

Chapter 4: Trading with Brands

Identifying brands that align with your image and values.

In the age of influencer marketing, many Youtubers and Influencers seek to work with brands that are aligned with their values and image. Working with brands that align with your content and personality can bring benefits to both sides, but identifying those brands can be challenging. In this article, we will discuss some strategies that Youtubers and Influencers can use to identify brands that align with their image and values.

Analyze your audience Before you start looking for brands to work with, it's important to understand your audience and what they value. Your audience is what drives your success, so it's important to know what they expect from you. What kind of products or services are they interested in? What motivates them to follow your channel or profile? By understanding your audience, you'll be able to identify brands that offer products or services that your followers want or need.

Identify your values and interests. It's important to have a clear idea of your values and interests, as this will help you identify brands that align with your image. For example, if you care about sustainability and the environment, you may want to work with brands that share these values. If you are passionate about fitness, you may want to work with brands that offer products or services related to this topic.

Research brands in your niche A good way to find brands that align with your image and values is to research other brands that are in your niche. What brands do your competitors work with? What are the popular brands in your niche? These brands may be interested in working with you as they already have a common interest.

Use influencer marketing platforms There are several influencer marketing platforms that can help you find brands that align with your image and values. These platforms connect Influencers with brands around the world. Some of these platforms include: BrandSnob, Influencer.co, HopperHQ, Klear and many others. It's important to note that some of these platforms charge a fee to use their services, so check the terms before signing up.

Contact brands directly if you already know which brands you want to work with, you can contact them directly. Make sure your message is professional and personalized. Explain why you believe your image and values align with those of the brand and how you can help promote it. Be prepared to provide statistics about your audience and engagement, as well as examples of previous successful campaigns.

Be open to new opportunities. While it's important to look for brands that align with your image and values, it's also important to be open to new opportunities. Working with brands outside of your niche can lead to new followers and growth opportunities. It's important to keep an open mind and evaluate each opportunity individually to determine if it fits your image and values, even if it's different from what you're used to.

Evaluate previous brand campaigns Before working with a brand, it's important to check your previous campaigns and assess whether they align with your image and values. Check if previous campaigns have been successful and if the brand works with other influencers in your niche. This will help ensure that collaboration is beneficial to both sides and that you are not promoting something that is not in line with your image or values.

Check brand reputation In addition to evaluating previous brand campaigns, it's important to check brand reputation. Check company reviews on review sites and social media to ensure the brand has a good reputation and is trustworthy. Working with brands with a bad reputation can damage your image and your followers' trust in you.

Keep in mind your long-term goals. When choosing brands to work with, it's important to keep in mind your long-term goals. What do you hope to achieve in the long term by working with these brands? Can they help increase your visibility and growth, or are you looking for more meaningful and lasting collaborations? Consider your long-term goals to ensure that the brands you choose can help achieve them.

Identifying brands that align with your image and values can be a challenging process, but it's important for success and authenticity in influencer marketing. Analyzing the audience, identifying values and interests, researching brands in the niche, using influencer marketing platforms, contacting brands directly, evaluating previous brand campaigns, verifying reputation, and keeping long-term goals in mind are useful strategies that Youtubers and Influencers can use to identify brands that align with their image and values.

Another important strategy to identify brands that align with your image and values is to look at social networks. Often, the brands you follow and like can follow back and interact with you. In addition, you can see the brands that your followers follow and which of them have positive interactions.

When working with brands, it's important that you are transparent and authentic with your audience. Followers expect you to promote only brands that align with your image and values, otherwise they may lose trust in you. Therefore, it's important that you select brands carefully and that you only work with those that you believe offer real value to your followers.

Also, when you work with a brand, make sure the campaign is authentic and relevant to your audience. Don't promote a product or service that isn't related to your niche or that you don't have personal experience with. Authenticity is the key to keeping your followers engaged and confident in you.

Finally, remember that influencer marketing is an ever-evolving industry. Brands and influencers are always looking for ways to stand out and innovate. Therefore, it is important to be open to new opportunities and be willing to try new things. The brands that align with your image and values now may not be the same ones that align in the future.

In short, identifying brands that align with your image and values is critical to influencer marketing success. By analyzing their audience, identifying their values and interests, researching brands in their niche, using influencer marketing platforms, contacting brands directly, and being open to new opportunities, Youtubers and Influencers can find the best brands to work with and establish lasting and authentic partnerships.

How to approach brands for partnerships and sponsorships

For many Youtubers and Influencers, collaborating with brands can be an important source of income and can also help expand their audience and increase their credibility. However, approaching brands for partnerships and sponsorships can be a challenging process. In this article, we'll discuss some strategies for approaching brands effectively and increasing the chances of success.

Research brands Before you approach a brand, it's important to do in-depth research on it. You must understand the brand's mission, values, target audience, products and services offered, as well as its presence on social networks. In addition, it is important to check if the brand has worked with Influencers in the past and has an established partnership program.

Create a media kit A media kit is a presentation that describes who you are, your content, your audience, and your accomplishments. This document can be sent to brands to help them understand their value as an Influencer. A media kit should include a brief biography, a description of your channel or profile, statistics about your audience, examples of content, previous work experience with other brands, and any other relevant information.

Contact the brand in a professional way when it comes to approaching brands, it is important to be professional and respectful. Make sure your message is personalized and explains why you want to work with that specific brand. In addition, it is important to provide specific examples of how you can help the brand achieve its goals. For example, you can explain how your content is relevant to the brand's target audience and how you can increase your social media presence.

Be clear about your expectations. When approaching a brand for partnerships or sponsorships, it's important to be clear about your expectations. For example, you can explain what your payment terms are, how many posts you will make, how long the campaign will last, what your requirements are for the content, and any other relevant information. Make sure your expectations are aligned with those of the brand.

Be open to negotiations. While it's important to be clear about your expectations, it's also important to be open to negotiations. Brands may have different ideas about the campaign, and it's important to be open to compromises that meet the needs of both parties. Make sure your initial expectations are realistic and that you are open to hearing the brand's opinion.

Track and analyze the results After closing a partnership or sponsorship with a brand, it is important to track and analyze the results of the campaign. Make sure that you are fulfilling all your obligations and that you are producing quality content for the brand. In addition, it's important to look at metrics, such as engagement and views, to understand the impact of the campaign.

Approaching brands for partnerships and sponsorships can be a challenging process, but by following these strategies, you can increase your chances of success. It's important to remember that approaching brands doesn't just mean seeking a source of income, but also establishing lasting relationships with brands relevant to your audience. By doing so, you can help increase your credibility and expand your reach.

Also, remember that transparency and honesty are key at every step of the process. Make sure you are being clear about your expectations and commitments, and that you are working ethically and professionally with brands. By doing so, you can establish a relationship of trust with brands and increase the chances of future collaborations.

Remember that success in approaching brands for partnerships and sponsorships takes time and effort. If a brand isn't interested in working with you, don't be discouraged. Keep creating quality content and developing your social media presence. Over time, you can increase your credibility and become a reference in your niche, which can help attract the attention of relevant brands.

Chapter 5: Engaging Your Community

How to interact with your followers and create a trusting relationship

For Youtubers and Influencers, interacting with followers is an essential part of maintaining an engaged audience and building a trusting relationship. In this article, we'll discuss some effective strategies for interacting with followers and creating a lasting relationship.

Respond to comments and messages: Responding to comments and messages from followers is one of the most basic, but effective, ways to interact with your audience. Answering questions and providing feedback can show followers that you value their opinion and that you care about connecting with them.

Conduct sweepstakes and contests: Conducting sweepstakes and contests can encourage follower participation and increase engagement with your content. These initiatives can help increase your channel's visibility and attract new followers.

Perform live and Q&A's: Holding live and Q&A sessions can create a more personal connection with followers. This allows them to communicate directly with you and start building a closer relationship.

Share user-generated content: Sharing user-generated content is a great way to engage the community and highlight your followers. This can encourage other followers to create and share content related to your channel or profile.

Create community groups: Creating community groups on social networks can help build a community around your content and allow followers to communicate with each other. This is a great way to create a space for relevant discussions and for followers to feel part of a community.

Hold meet and greets and live events: Holding meet and greets and live events can allow followers to connect personally with you and other followers. This can create a sense of belonging to the community and increase the loyalty of followers.

Include calls-to-action in your videos: Including calls-to-action in your videos can encourage followers to engage with you and your content. This may include requests for followers to comment, share, or like the videos.

Maintain consistency: It's important to maintain a consistent content publishing schedule to keep your audience engaged and build a trusting relationship. This can include regularly posting to stories, updating followers on the content publishing schedule, and maintaining an active social media presence.

Interacting with followers is an essential part of the success of Youtubers and Influencers. These strategies can help build a trusting relationship with your audience, encourage engagement, and build community around your content. It's important to be consistent and take the time to connect with followers in an authentic and meaningful way.

Another effective strategy for interacting with followers is personalization. Showing interest in followers and their lives can make them feel valued and connected with you. You can do this by mentioning them in your videos, asking about their interests or hobbies, and answering their questions in a personalized way.

It's also important to be authentic and transparent with followers. Sharing your personal experiences and showing vulnerability can help create an emotional connection with your audience. This may include talking about your personal or professional challenges and how you overcame those obstacles.

In addition, creating a sense of purpose and mission can help inspire and engage followers. This may include talking about your passions and why you're creating content for your channel or profile. Communicating a clear and cohesive message can make followers identify with you and feel part of a larger cause.

Finally, being mindful of trends and the interests of followers can help create more relevant and engaging content. This can include keeping up with current news and events, as well as trends on social media and in your niche market. Creating content that meets the needs and interests of followers can help increase audience engagement and loyalty.

In short, interacting with followers is key to creating a relationship of trust and lasting engagement. The strategies mentioned in this article, such as responding to comments and messages, conducting sweepstakes and contests, performing live and Q&A's, sharing user-generated content, and creating community groups, can help build a community around your content. In addition, being authentic, transparent, and having a sense of purpose can inspire and engage followers. Finally, being mindful of trends and the interests of followers can help create more relevant and engaging content.

Strategies to increase audience engagement and loyalty.

For Youtubers and Influencers, increasing audience engagement and loyalty is essential for long-term success. In this article, we will discuss some effective strategies for increasing audience engagement and loyalty.

Create quality content: The quality of the content is key to keeping the audience interested and engaged. This includes producing high-quality content that meets your audience's expectations and is relevant to them.

Foster interaction: Encourage your audience to engage with content by asking questions, encouraging comments, and sharing. Be sure to answer all questions and comments, so that the audience feels that your opinions are valued.

Be authentic: Followers are more likely to engage with an influencer who is authentic and genuine. Show your personality and let followers know the real you.

Use social media: social media is a great way to connect with your audience. Be sure to post regularly on social media and create unique content for each platform.

Collaborate with other influencers: Collaborations with other influencers can help increase the visibility of your content and expand your audience. Look for influencers who share similar interests and who have an audience like yours.

Offer unique content: Offer unique content to your followers, such as webinars, tutorials, and interviews. This can increase audience loyalty, making them feel privileged to have access to exclusive content.

Conduct sweepstakes and contests: Conducting sweepstakes and contests can encourage follower participation and increase engagement with your content. These initiatives can help increase your channel's visibility and attract new followers.

Hold live events: Hosting live events can allow followers to connect in person with you and other followers. This can create a sense of belonging to the community and increase the loyalty of followers.

Offer rewards: Offering rewards to the most engaged followers can encourage engagement and increase audience loyalty. This can include the inclusion of followers in videos, exclusive sweepstakes, or the possibility of having direct contact with the influencer.

Be consistent: It's important to maintain a consistent content publishing schedule to keep your audience engaged and build a relationship of trust. This can include regularly posting to stories, updating followers on the content publishing schedule, and maintaining an active social media presence.

In conclusion, increasing audience engagement and loyalty is critical to the success of Youtubers and Influencers. These strategies can help create a trusting relationship with your audience by encouraging participation and building an engaged community around your content. By following these strategies, Youtubers and Influencers can grow their audience, create a stronger relationship with the audience and ensure long-term success.

However, it's important to remember that building an engaged and loyal audience takes time and effort. It is necessary to be consistent and dedicated in producing high-quality content and interacting with the audience. It is essential to know your audience and adapt your strategy according to their needs and interests.

In addition, it is important not to fall into the trap of focusing only on numbers, such as the number of followers or views. While these metrics are important, true success should be measured by the quality of your relationship with your audience and your ability to influence and inspire people.

In summary, strategies to increase audience engagement and loyalty include creating quality content, fostering interaction, authenticity, using social media, collaborating with other influencers, offering exclusive content, conducting sweepstakes and contests, holding live events, offering rewards, and consistency in content production. By following these strategies and dedicating themselves to the relationship with the public, Youtubers and Influencers can build an engaged and loyal community around their content.

How to deal with negative comments and manage reputation crises.

For Youtubers and Influencers, dealing with negative comments and managing reputation crises can be a challenging part of the job. However, it is critical to learn how to handle these situations to maintain a positive reputation and ensure long-term success. In this article, we'll discuss some strategies for dealing with negative comments and managing reputation crises.

Monitor your online presence: It is important to regularly monitor your online presence to quickly identify any negative comments or criticisms. You can use social media monitoring tools to track mentions of your name and your channel or profile. Keeping an eye on this information allows you to respond quickly and reduce the negative impact.

Keep calm: It's critical to stay calm and not let negative comments affect you personally. Responding with anger or frustration only makes the situation worse and can affect your reputation. Instead, try to respond politely and professionally, explaining your position or offering a solution to the problem presented.

Respond quickly: Responding quickly to negative comments is important to minimize damage to your reputation. This shows that you are committed to solving the problem and can help calm the situation before it gets worse. If necessary, apologize for the problem or error and offer a solution to fix it.

Don't ignore negative comments: Ignoring negative comments can make the situation worse and affect your reputation. Instead, try to respond to all comments, even negative ones. This shows that you care about your audience's opinion and are willing to solve any problem that may arise.

Take the conversation to a private environment: In some cases, it may be best to take the conversation to a private environment, such as by email or direct message on social networks. This allows you to solve the problem without exposing the audience to a negative discussion. Remember to always maintain education and professionalism in these conversations.

Ask for professional help if needed: If the reputation crisis is too great or you don't know how to handle the situation, it's important to ask for professional help. You can hire a reputation management agency to help deal with the crisis and regain your reputation.

Do not defend yourself too much: While it's important to respond to negative comments, it's important not to overdefend yourself. This can be interpreted as defensive and can make the situation worse. Instead, be polite and offer a solution to the problem presented.

Be transparent: Being transparent with your audience is key to building a relationship of trust. If you make a mistake, admit it and apologize. If you are dealing with a reputation crisis, explain the situation clearly and honestly.

Do not buy positive reviews: Buying positive reviews to improve your reputation is unethical and can damage your credibility. In addition, followers may realize that these comments are fake, and this can further damage their reputation. Instead, focus on creating authentic, quality content that will naturally attract positive feedback.

Learn from mistakes: Instead of focusing only on the negatives, try to learn from the mistakes and negative feedback you receive. This can help you improve your content and avoid similar problems in the future.

Dealing with negative comments and managing reputation crises can be challenging for Youtubers and Influencers. However, it is important to remember that these situations can happen to anyone on the internet and that how you deal with them can have a significant impact on your reputation eventually. So, monitor your online presence, stay calm, respond quickly, do not ignore negative comments, take the conversation to a private setting if needed, ask for professional help if needed, be transparent, don't overdefend yourself, don't buy positive comments and learn from mistakes. Following these strategies can help you deal with negative comments and reputation crises in a professional manner and build a positive reputation on the internet.

Chapter 6: Content Monetization

Strategies to make money with your social networks.

With the popularization of social networks, many Youtubers and Influencers have been looking for ways to monetize their online platforms. There are several strategies to make money with your social networks, from paid advertising to the sale of your own products or services. In this article, we will introduce you to some of the top strategies for monetizing your social networks.

Paid advertising: One of the most common ways to make money from your social networks is through paid advertising. Companies pay to have their brands or products advertised by influencers who have a large number of followers. It is important, however, that the publications are in line with the content of the Influencer and that followers perceive advertising in a natural and not forced way.

Affiliate programs: Affiliate programs are another fashionable way to monetize your social networks. In this model, Influencer promotes products or services from other companies in their publications and receives a commission on the sales generated from their affiliate link. It is important to choose products or services that are in line with the content of the Influencer and that have sales potential among your followers.

Sponsorships: Sponsorships are agreements between the Influencer and a brand, in which the Influencer promotes the brand's products or services in its publications for a certain period in exchange for financial compensation. This strategy can be quite profitable, but it is important to choose brands that are aligned with the content and values of the Influencer so that the promotion feels natural.

Selling your own products or services: Another way to monetize your social networks is through the sale of your own products or services. If the Influencer has an engaged audience and interested in your content, you can create digital products such as e-books, online courses, workshops, or other products that can be sold directly to followers. In addition, you can use social networks to promote physical products, such as clothing, accessories or other items that are related to the content of the Influencer.

Events: Holding in-person or online events can be another interesting way to monetize social networks. If the Influencer has an engaged and loyal audience, it is possible to organize meetings, meet & greets, lectures or other events that allow direct contact with followers. In addition, it is possible to organize online events, such as webinars or workshops, and charge for participation or exclusive content.

Donations: Some social networks allow followers to make donations to content creators. This strategy can be used by Influencers who have an engaged community willing to contribute financially to the development of the content. It is important, however, that this donation option is presented transparently and without forcing the bar.

In summary, there are several strategies to make money with your social networks. It is important that the Influencer chooses those that are in line with your content and that can generate value for your followers. In addition, it is essential to maintain transparency and authenticity in all publications, avoiding promoting products or services that are not relevant or of dubious quality.

Another crucial point is to have a clear content and publications strategy to keep your followers engaged and interested in your profile. You need to create a trusting relationship with the audience so that monetization strategies do not seem invasive or uninteresting.

Finally, it is important to highlight that monetizing social networks requires work and dedication on the part of the Influencer. It is necessary to produce quality content, keep up to date on the trends and news of the platform, and always be attentive to the needs and interests of followers.

In short, social networks offer several opportunities for Youtubers and Influencers to make money and monetize their online platforms. It is important to choose the strategies that best suit the profile and content of the Influencer, always maintaining transparency, authenticity, and quality in publications.

How to Create Sponsored Content Without Harming Your Brand Image

Youtubers and Influencers have become increasingly popular and, consequently, attractive to brands looking to promote their products or services. However, care must be taken that sponsored content does not harm the Influencer's brand image. In this article, we will present some tips for creating sponsored content to preserve brand image.

Choosing brands that are aligned with your content is important that the brands you choose are in line with the content and values of the Influencer. Otherwise, the promotion may seem forced and misaligned with the rest of the content, which can damage the Influencer's brand image. It is important to remember that credibility is one of the main assets of the Influencer and, therefore, must be preserved.

Be transparent with your followers Transparency is key to maintaining followers' trust. It is necessary to make it clear that this is sponsored content and that the Influencer is being remunerated for the promotion of the brand. You can do this discreetly, using hashtags such as #publi, #ad or #patrocinado, for example.

Do not compromise the quality of the content Sponsored content should not compromise the quality of the Influencer's content. It is important to maintain the authenticity and originality of the content, even when it's a promotion. The Influencer can, for example, create brand-specific content that is in line with the rest of the content and that is interesting to followers.

Be creative and authentic Creativity and authenticity are important to ensure that sponsored content does not feel forced or uninteresting. The Influencer can use their creativity to create content that is attractive and that is in line with their style and brand message.

Do not promote products or services you don't know. It is important that the Influencer knows well the product or service they are promoting. Otherwise, it may convey an image of lack of authenticity and credibility. You need to try the product or service before promoting it and evaluate whether it really is relevant to the audience and is in line with the content of the Influencer.

Maintain ethics The Influencer must maintain ethics in their promotions and avoid, for example, making misleading statements or promises that cannot be fulfilled. It is important that the promotion is honest and transparent, so that followers can make their own decisions based on truthful information.

In short, you can create sponsored content to preserve the Influencer's brand image. For this, it is important to choose brands aligned with the content, be transparent with followers, not compromise the quality of the content, be creative and authentic, promote only products or services that you know and maintain ethics in your promotions. Thus, the Influencer can continue to build an image of credibility and trust among their followers, even when it comes to sponsored content. It is important to remember that the brand image of the Influencer is a valuable asset and must be preserved carefully so that the relationship with followers is not harmed.

In addition to these tips, it is important to note that the legislation regarding sponsored content may vary from country to country. It is important that the Influencer is aware of local laws and regulations regarding this type of content, to avoid legal problems or fines.

Finally, it is important to remember that sponsored content doesn't have to be seen as something negative. When done ethically and transparently, it can be a way to generate revenue and offer followers access to products and services that may be relevant to them. With the tips presented in this article, it is possible to create sponsored content that benefits both the Influencer and the brand, without compromising the Influencer's brand image.

Maximizing your monetization opportunities

As a Youtuber or Influencer, you can make money from your content through different forms of monetization. In this article, we'll discuss some of the top strategies for maximizing your monetization opportunities.

Advertising is one of the most common forms of monetization for Youtubers and Influencers. AdSense allows you to show ads on your YouTube videos and pay per click or view. However, the amount you get can vary, depending on your channel's niche, audience, and engagement.

Another option is direct advertising, where brands pay directly for you to feature their products or services on your channel. It is important to make sure these promotions are relevant to your audience and are in line with your personal brand, to avoid a loss of credibility.

Affiliate marketing Affiliate marketing is a popular form of monetization that involves promoting products or services from other companies. When a follower clicks on your affiliate link and makes a purchase, you receive a commission on the sale. It is important to choose products and services that are in line with your channel's content and that are relevant to your audience.

Sponsorship is another form of monetization that involves collaborating with brands to promote their products or services. These collaborations can range from one-off agreements to long-term contracts and usually involve paying a fixed amount or a percentage of the sales generated from the promotion. It is important to choose brands that are aligned with your values and goals to maintain the authenticity of your content.

Sale of products or services the sale of own products or services can also be a form of monetization for Youtubers and Influencers. This can range from digital products, such as e-books and online courses, to physical products, such as clothing and accessories. It is important to remember that the success of this strategy depends on the development of a loyal and engaged audience.

Crowdfunding is a crowdfunding strategy in which followers contribute financially to support the work of the Youtuber or Influencer. Crowdfunding platforms such as Patreon allow followers to support their favorite content creators through monthly payments or for specific content. It is important to offer attractive rewards to encourage people to contribute.

Live events. Live events, such as concerts, fan meetings, and workshops, can be another form of monetization for Youtubers and Influencers. These events allow followers to connect in person with their favorite creators and are often charged per ticket. It is important to ensure that these events are well planned and promoted to attract a significant audience.

In summary, there are several monetization strategies available for Youtubers and Influencers. It is important to experiment with different ways and find the ones that best suit your niche, your audience, and your style. In addition, it is essential to maintain the quality and authenticity of your content to maintain audience loyalty and engagement.

However, to maximize your monetization opportunities, it is important to invest in an effective marketing strategy. This involves creating a strong and coherent brand, building a loyal and engaged audience, and constantly promoting your channel and content on social media and other relevant online platforms.

In addition, it is important to closely monitor the results of your monetization strategies and make adjustments as needed. This may involve testing different ad formats, adjusting your affiliate marketing tactics, or seeking new sponsorship partnerships.

In conclusion, maximizing monetization opportunities as a Youtuber or Influencer involves combining various strategies, including advertising, affiliate marketing, sponsorship, selling products or services, crowdfunding, and live events. By investing in an effective marketing strategy and maintaining the quality and authenticity of your content, you can increase your chances of success and achieving your financial goals.

Chapter 7: Data Analysis and Metrics

How to Measure the Performance and Success of Your Influencer Marketing Campaigns

Influencer Marketing has become a popular strategy for brands to reach wider audiences, and many Youtubers and Influencers use this form of monetization to earn income. However, it is essential to measure the performance and success of your Influencer Marketing campaigns to know if you are having the expected return. In this article, we will discuss some of the key metrics for measuring the performance and success of your Influencer Marketing campaigns.

Reach is one of the most important metrics for measuring the performance of an Influencer Marketing campaign. Reach measures how many people have been exposed to campaign content, and can be calculated by the number of views, shares, and interactions. It is important to keep in mind that reach does not always translate into engagement or conversion, but it's an important metric for evaluating campaign visibility.

Engagement is another important metric for measuring the performance of an Influencer Marketing campaign. Engagement measures the interaction of followers with the content of the campaign, and can be calculated through the number of likes, comments, and shares. A high engagement indicates that the campaign was well received by the public and that it generated interest and interaction. However, engagement can also be influenced by other factors, such as the platform's algorithm and content quality.

Conversion is the most important metric for measuring the success of an Influencer Marketing campaign. Conversion measures how many followers who were exposed to campaign content took the desired action, such as making a purchase or subscribing to an email list. The conversion can be calculated through the number of clicks on the campaign link and the sales made from that link. It's important to remember that conversion can be influenced by a number of factors, such as product price, content quality, and follower trust in the brand.

ROI (Return on Investment) is an important metric for measuring the financial success of an Influencer Marketing campaign. ROI measures the financial return generated by the campaign in relation to the investment made by the brand. ROI can be calculated by subtracting the cost of the campaign from the gain generated by the campaign, divided by the cost of the campaign. A positive ROI indicates that the campaign generated a profit for the brand, while a negative ROI indicates that the campaign generated a loss.

Customer satisfaction. Customer satisfaction is an important metric for measuring the long-term success of an influencer marketing campaign. Customer satisfaction measures the level of satisfaction of customers who purchased the product or service promoted in the campaign. It's important to remember that customer satisfaction can influence customer loyalty and return on investment for the brand in the long run.

In summary, measuring the performance and success of an Influencer Marketing campaign is essential to understand if you are achieving the expected return and justify the brand's investment. For this, it is important to consider various metrics such as reach, engagement, conversion, ROI, and customer satisfaction.

Reach measures how many people have been exposed to campaign content, while engagement measures followers' interaction with the content. Conversion is the most important metric as it measures how many followers who were exposed to the content took the desired action. ROI is key to evaluating the financial success of the campaign and measuring the return on investment. Finally, customer satisfaction is important for assessing the long-term impact of the campaign on customer loyalty and return on investment.

By measuring these metrics, you can measure the success of an Influencer Marketing campaign and identify areas that can be improved to increase the brand's return on investment. It is important to remember that these metrics should be evaluated together, as each provides a different perspective on campaign performance.

Identifying important metrics for Youtubers and Influencers

Youtubers and Influencers need to identify the most important metrics for the success of their marketing and monetization activities. Metrics are important indicators for evaluating audience performance, engagement, conversion, and loyalty. In this article, we will discuss some of the most important metrics for Youtubers and Influencers.

Scope

Reach measures how many people have been exposed to Youtuber or Influencer content and can be measured through views, shares, and interactions. Reach is a key metric for assessing channel and campaign visibility. Reach can be maximized through SEO techniques and promotion on social platforms.

Commitment

Engagement is a metric that measures audience interaction with Youtuber or Influencer content. Engagement can be measured through likes, comments, shares, and subscriptions. Engagement is an important indicator to assess the level of interest and engagement of the audience with the channel or campaign. High engagement indicates that the audience is interested and engaged with the content and brand.

Audience retention

Audience retention measures the viewing rate of a video relative to the total time of the video. Audience retention is important to evaluate the quality of the content and the ability of the Youtuber or Influencer to maintain the interest of the public. A high retention rate indicates that the audience is watching the content longer and is interested in what is being presented.

Conversion

The conversion measures how many followers have taken the action desired by the Youtuber or Influencer, such as making a purchase or subscribing to an email list. The conversion can be calculated through the number of clicks on the campaign link and the sales made from that link. Conversion is important to assess the ability of the Youtuber or Influencer to influence the audience to take a specific action. It's important to remember that conversion can be influenced by a number of factors, such as product price, content quality, and follower trust in the brand.

Revenue

Revenue is an important financial metric for Youtubers and Influencers. Revenue is generated through channel monetization, sponsorships, and Influencer Marketing campaigns. Revenue is an important indicator of the financial success of the channel and the ability of the Youtuber or Influencer to monetize your content and your audience.

ROI (Return on Investment) is an important financial metric for Youtubers and Influencers. ROI measures the financial return generated in relation to the investment made. ROI can be calculated by subtracting the cost of the campaign from the gain generated by the campaign, divided by the cost of the campaign. A positive ROI indicates that the campaign generated a profit for the Youtuber or Influencer, while a negative ROI indicates that the campaign generated a loss.

Public satisfaction

Audience satisfaction is a metric that measures the level of audience satisfaction and loyalty to content and brand. Audience satisfaction can be measured through opinion polls, reviews, and feedback. It is important to remember that audience satisfaction is related to the quality of the content, the relevance of the message and the coherence of the brand. Audience satisfaction is an important indicator to assess the health of the channel and the longevity of the audience.

Conclusion

Identifying the most important metrics for Youtubers and Influencers is key to evaluating the performance, effectiveness and profitability of the channel and campaign. Metrics should be selected based on the objectives and needs of the Youtuber or Influencer, as well as the Marketing strategy adopted. Metrics can be monitored through data analysis tools and through direct feedback from the public. It is important to remember that metrics should be evaluated regularly so that they can be adjusted and optimized according to the needs and challenges of the channel and campaign.

Using data to improve your marketing strategies.

Youtubers and Influencers can use data to improve their marketing strategies and maximize the success of their activities. Data can be collected from a variety of sources, including the metrics mentioned earlier, and analyzed to identify trends and patterns of audience behavior.

Audience targeting

One of the main ways to use data to improve marketing strategies is through audience segmentation. Audience segmentation involves dividing the audience into groups with similar characteristics, such as age, gender, location, interests, and behaviors. By segmenting the audience, the Youtuber or Influencer can create specific content and campaigns for each group, increasing the relevance and effectiveness of your marketing.

A/B testing

Another way to use data to improve marketing strategies is through A/B testing. A/B testing involves creating two versions of a campaign or content, with only one variable being changed between them, and distributing those versions to a sample audience. The results are measured and compared to determine which version is most effective in achieving the desired goal. A/B testing can be used to evaluate different titles, images, calls to action, pricing, and more.

Customization

The data can also be used to personalize content and campaigns for everyone. By collecting audience data such as browsing history, past purchases, and social media interactions, the Youtuber or Influencer can create personalized content and campaigns for each follower. Personalization increases audience relevance and interest in content, increasing the likelihood of conversion and loyalty.

Trend analysis

Trend analysis is another way to use data to improve marketing strategies. Trend analysis involves analyzing data over time to identify patterns and trends in audience behavior. This can include seasonal trends such as increased sales at Christmas or falling views during the holidays, as well as long-term trends such as increased use of smartphones for video viewing. With this information, the Youtuber or Influencer can adapt their strategies to take advantage of these trends and maximize their success.

Competitor tracking

The data can also be used to track and evaluate competition. Through the analysis of competitors' metrics and marketing strategies, the Youtuber or Influencer can identify opportunities and threats for their own channel and campaigns. This can include identifying gaps in the market or successful strategies used by competitors.

In short, Youtubers and Influencers can use data to improve their marketing strategies in a variety of ways, including audience segmentation, A/B testing, personalization, trend analysis, and competitor tracking. Data collection and analysis are key to maximizing the success of marketing and monetization activities, allowing Youtubers and Influencers to make more informed and strategic decisions. By using data, you can optimize content and campaigns to meet your audience's needs and interests, increase engagement and conversion, and outperform the competition.

It is important to note that the privacy of the public must be considered when collecting and using data. Youtubers and Influencers must ensure that they comply with privacy laws and obtain the public's consent for the collection and use of their data.

In addition, it is essential that Youtubers and Influencers have a solid understanding of the data and metrics used in their marketing strategies. They should know what data to collect, how to interpret it, and how to use it effectively. This may require hiring data analytics professionals or participating in courses and training to enhance skills in this area.

In conclusion, data collection and analysis are valuable tools for Youtubers and Influencers to improve their marketing strategies. By segmenting audiences, A/B testing, personalizing content, analyzing trends, and tracking competition, they can maximize the success of their marketing and monetization activities. However, it is important to stress that the privacy of the public must be protected and that it is essential to have a solid knowledge about data and metrics to use it effectively.

Chapter 8: New Trends in Influencer Marketing

Emerging Trends in Influencer Marketing

Influencer marketing has been a key tool for many brands and companies in recent years, especially regarding the use of Youtubers and Influencers to promote products and services. With the advancement of technology and the emergence of current trends, it is important that Youtubers and Influencers are aware of emerging trends in influencer marketing to maximize the success of their activities. Below are some emerging trends that are shaping the future of influencer marketing.

Micro-Influencers

One of the emerging trends in influencer marketing is the use of micro-influencers. Micro-influencers are individuals with a smaller number of followers, usually between 1,000 and 10,000, but with a high level of engagement in their community. Due to their more modest size, micro-influencers are often more accessible and authentic, which can generate greater trust and credibility with the public. This trend is gaining popularity because brands are realizing that engagement is more important than audience size when it comes to achieving marketing goals.

TikTok

Another emerging trend in influencer marketing is the use of TikTok. TikTok is a short-lived video platform that allows users to create and share fun and creative videos. Since its launch in 2016, TikTok has become one of the most popular social media platforms worldwide, especially among younger audiences. TikTok offers a unique opportunity for Youtubers and Influencers to reach a new audience and create creative and authentic content that can drive meaningful engagement.

Purpose Marketing

Purpose marketing is another emerging trend in influencer marketing. Purpose marketing is the practice of associating a brand or product with a social or environmental cause. This may include using sustainable materials, donating a portion of sales to a social cause, or sponsoring events related to social causes. Consumers are increasingly interested in brands that have a purpose and that are socially and environmentally responsible, and this can be an opportunity for Youtubers and Influencers to align their marketing activities with relevant social causes.

Virtual reality

Virtual reality is another emerging trend in influencer marketing. Virtual reality allows users to experience products and services in an immersive virtual environment. This can include using virtual reality technology to simulate the use of a product or service in a virtual environment. Virtual reality can be an innovative way for brands and companies to promote their products and services in a creative and engaging way.

Artificial intelligence

Artificial intelligence is another emerging trend in influencer marketing. Artificial intelligence can be used to analyze data and identify patterns of audience behavior, allowing Youtubers and Influencers to adjust their marketing strategies based on accurate information. Artificial intelligence can also be used to create personalized content for everyone based on their preferences and interests, which can increase audience engagement with the content.

In addition, artificial intelligence can be used to identify fake news and false information, which is especially important in influencer marketing, where credibility and trust are key to success. Artificial intelligence can also help Youtubers and Influencers manage and analyze their social networks more efficiently, saving them time and allowing them to focus on creating high-quality content.

Influencer marketing is a powerful tool for brands and companies to reach and engage their target audience. With emerging trends shaping the future of influencer marketing, Youtubers and Influencers need to be mindful and adapt their strategies to maximize the success of their activities. By using micro-influencers, TikTok, purposeful marketing, virtual reality, and artificial intelligence, Youtubers and Influencers can create more authentic, engaging and effective content, establishing a relationship of trust and credibility with their audience and increasing the impact of their marketing activities.

How to keep up to date with changes in the market

For Youtubers and Influencers, keeping up to date with changes in the market is essential to achieving and maintaining success in influencer marketing. In this article, we will cover some effective strategies for keeping up to date with changes in the market.

Attend conferences and events.

Attending conferences and events related to your niche market is an excellent way to stay up to date with the latest trends. These events allow you to meet other industry professionals, learn from experienced speakers, and discover new ideas and solutions for your business. By attending these events, you can also meet new business partners and collaborators.

Read specialized publications.

Reading specialized publications is an effective way to stay up to date with changes in the market. There are many specialized magazines and websites that cover influencer marketing and other topics relevant to Youtubers and Influencers. These publications provide insights into the latest trends, marketing strategies, and essential information about competitors. In addition, they can also provide valuable information about recent technologies and tools that can help you improve your social media presence.

Join online discussion groups.

Participating in online discussion groups is another way to stay up to date with changes in the market. These groups are an excellent source of information on the latest trends, marketing tips, and successful strategies. In addition, you can also ask questions, share your own ideas, and collaborate with other industry professionals.

Keep up with influencers and competitors.

Keeping up with influencers and competitors is another way to stay up to date with changes in the market. By following the influencers in your niche, you can discover current trends, see how they are working to stand out, and learn from your marketing strategies. In addition, monitoring your competitors can provide valuable insight into the marketing strategies they are using and emerging trends in the market.

Use data analysis tools.

Using data analysis tools is another way to stay up to date with changes in the market. There are many tools available that can help you monitor the performance of your influencer marketing campaigns, analyze market trends, and uncover growth opportunities. These tools can also help you understand your target audience's behavior and identify new opportunities for collaboration with other influencers.

Keeping up to date with changes in the market is crucial for Youtubers and Influencers who want to achieve and maintain success in influencer marketing. Attending conferences and events, reading specialized publications, participating in online discussion groups, keeping up with influencers and competitors, and using data analytics tools are some of the most effective ways to stay up to date with changes in the market. It is important to remember that the influencer marketing market is constantly evolving, so it is critical to always be up to date to stay relevant and competitive.

In addition, it is important to be open to current ideas and changes. As recent technologies and trends emerge, it is important to adapt your influencer marketing strategy and find ways to incorporate these changes into your campaigns. Keeping up to date with changes in the market can be challenging, but it is a valuable investment for long-term success in influencer marketing.

Finally, it is worth emphasizing the importance of seeking constant knowledge and learning. Attending online courses, taking training, and learning from experienced professionals can also be a wonderful way to stay up to date and hone your skills. The influencer marketing market is highly competitive and those who are always looking to evolve and improve themselves have a significant advantage.

Preparing for the Future of Influencer Marketing

Influencer marketing has grown exponentially in recent years and the trend is that it will continue to grow in the future. Therefore, it is important that Youtubers and Influencers are prepared to face the changes that will come. In this article, we'll cover some strategies for preparing for the future of influencer marketing.

Stay up to date with consumer trends One of the key trends in influencer marketing is the growing concern with social and environmental issues. Consumers are more aware of the ethical and sustainable practices of brands and expect influencers to engage in these issues as well. Therefore, it is important that Youtubers and Influencers are aware of consumer trends and adopt ethical and sustainable practices in their work.

Diversify your communication channels today, YouTube is the main platform for influencers, but this may change in the future. Therefore, it is important that Youtubers and Influencers diversify their communication channels and are present on other platforms, such as Instagram, TikTok and Twitch. In this way, they can reach different audiences and adapt to changes in consumer behavior.

Invest in quality content Quality content has always been key in influencer marketing and that should not change in the future. Consumers are increasingly demanding and expect relevant and authentic content from influencers. Therefore, it is important that Youtubers and Influencers invest in quality content that adds value to their followers and is consistent with their values and personality.

Strengthen your personal brand with the increase in the number of influencers, it is important that Youtubers and Influencers strengthen their personal brand to stand out in the market. This includes defining a cohesive visual identity, creating a unique tone of voice, and establishing an emotional connection with your followers. In addition, it is important that they invest in their personal and professional development to enhance their skills and knowledge.

Look for more strategic partnerships. Partnerships have always been an important part of influencer marketing, but in the future, they tend to become even more strategic. Brands are increasingly demanding and expect more concrete results from influencers. Therefore, it is important that Youtubers and Influencers seek more strategic partnerships, which are aligned with their values and goals, and that allow a deeper and more lasting work with brands.

Influencer marketing will continue to grow in the future and Youtubers and Influencers must be prepared to face the changes that will come. By keeping up to date with consumer trends, diversifying their communication channels, investing in quality content, strengthening their personal brand, and seeking more strategic partnerships, they can ensure their success in the influencer market. In addition, it is important that they are always open to learning and adapting to changes, as influencer marketing is constantly evolving and those who do not adapt are left behind. It is also necessary for them to be transparent and honest with their audience and their partnerships, maintaining ethics and integrity in their work as influencers.

Another important trend in influencer marketing is the use of modern technologies such as artificial intelligence and virtual reality. Youtubers and Influencers must be aware of these novelties and adapt to them, incorporating them into their work in a creative and innovative way.

Finally, it is important to point out that success in influencer marketing depends not only on the number of followers, but also on the quality of the influencer's work and the engagement of his audience. Therefore, it is essential that Youtubers and Influencers build a solid and trusting relationship with their followers, interacting with them in an authentic and true way.

In summary, to prepare for the future of influencer marketing, Youtubers and Influencers must be up to date with consumer trends, diversify their communication channels, invest in quality content, strengthen their personal brand, seek more strategic partnerships and be open to new technologies. In addition, it is critical that they build a solid and authentic relationship with their followers and are transparent and ethical in their work as influencers.